THE ULTIMATE
HOW TO DRAW
CUTE STUFF BOOK

Check us out on youtube @**Ultimate Kid Press Channel**
Share your art on facebook @**ultimatekidpress**
Let us know what you think!
Leave us a review

© ULTIMATE KID PRESS

HOW TO USE THIS BOOK

1: GET A PENCIL, ERASER, AND MARKERS
2: FIND SOMETHING CUTE AND AWESOME
3: DRAW THE RED LINES FROM EACH STEP
4: AS YOU GO ERASE THE GREY LINES
5: OUTLINE WITH MARKER AND COLOR IN
6: IF YOU MAKE A MISTAKE JUST TRY AGAIN
   (PRACTICE MAKES PERFECT)

TABLE OF CONTENTS

CUPCAKE

PIZZA

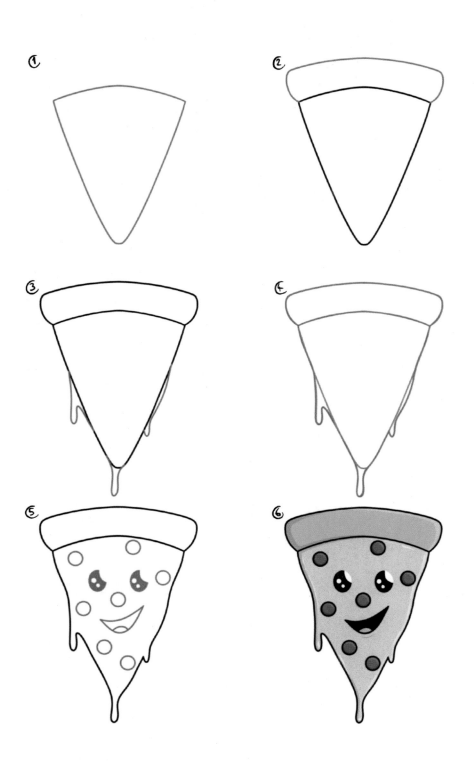

FRIES

1

2

3

4

5

6

BURGER

COFFEE

①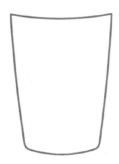

②

③

④

⑤

⑥

POPSICLE

BOBA

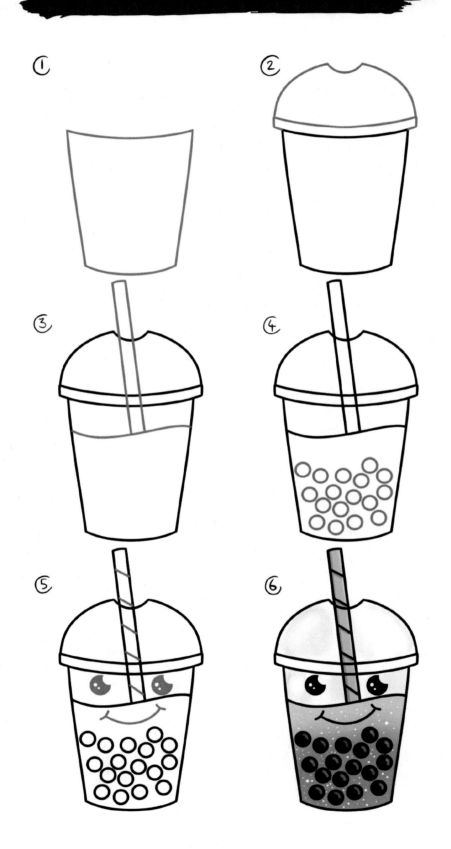

WAFFLE

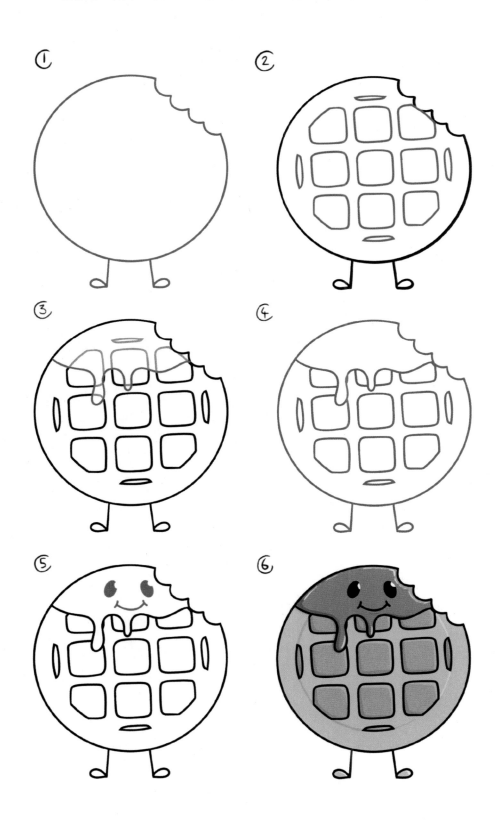

ICE CREAM

ICE CREAM

TACO

STRAWBERRY

CANDY BAR

PINEAPPLE

SUSHI

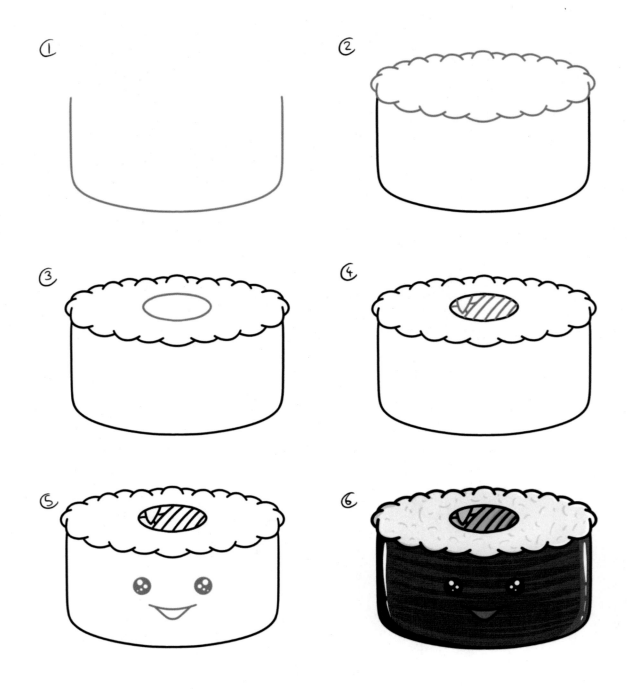

SWISS ROLL

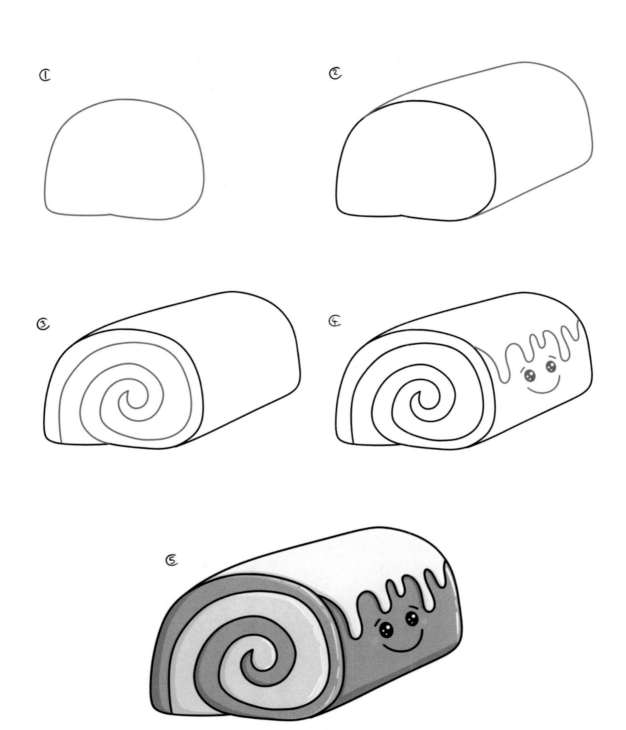

EGGS & BACON

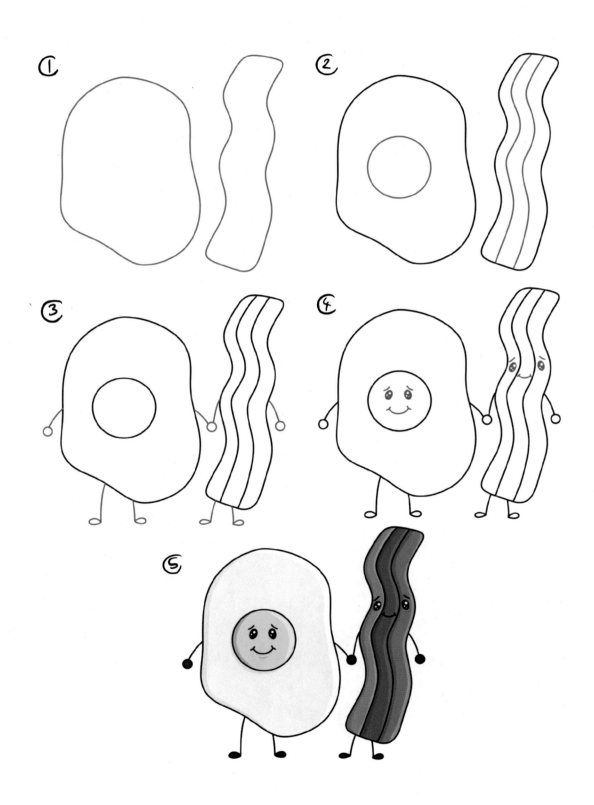

CINNAMON ROLL

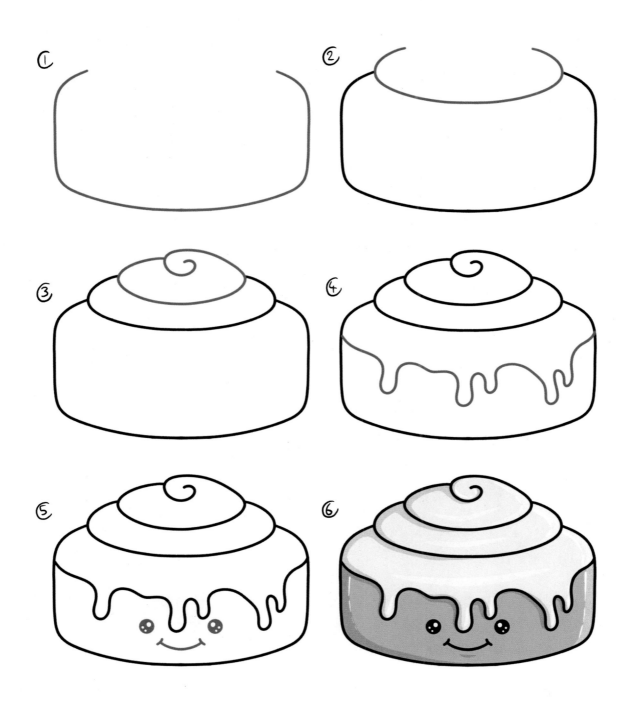

WATERMELON

BURRITO

CATICORN

①

②

③

④

CATICORN

PENCIL

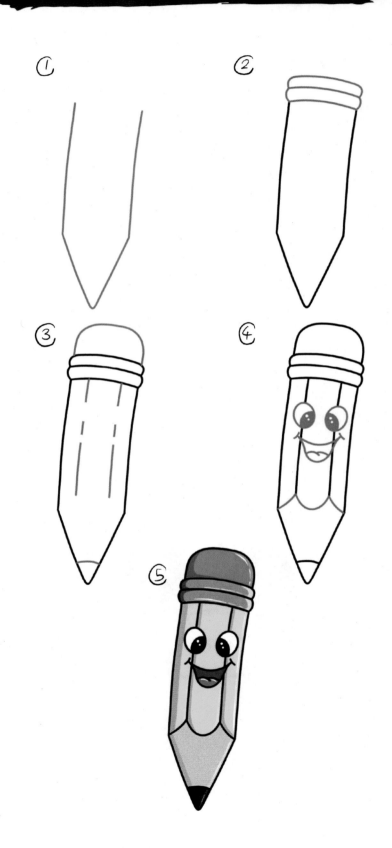

① ② ③ ④ ⑤

TOASTER

①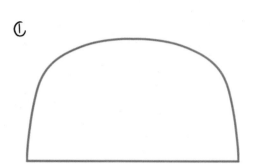

②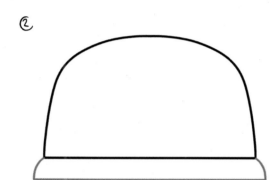

③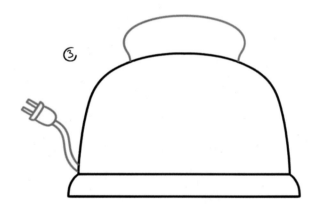

④

⑤

KITTIES

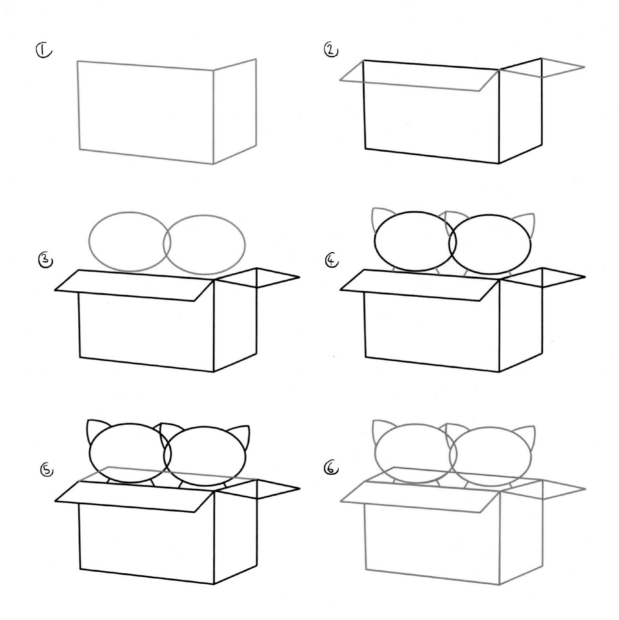

① ② ③ ④ ⑤ ⑥

KITTIES

SUNGLASSES

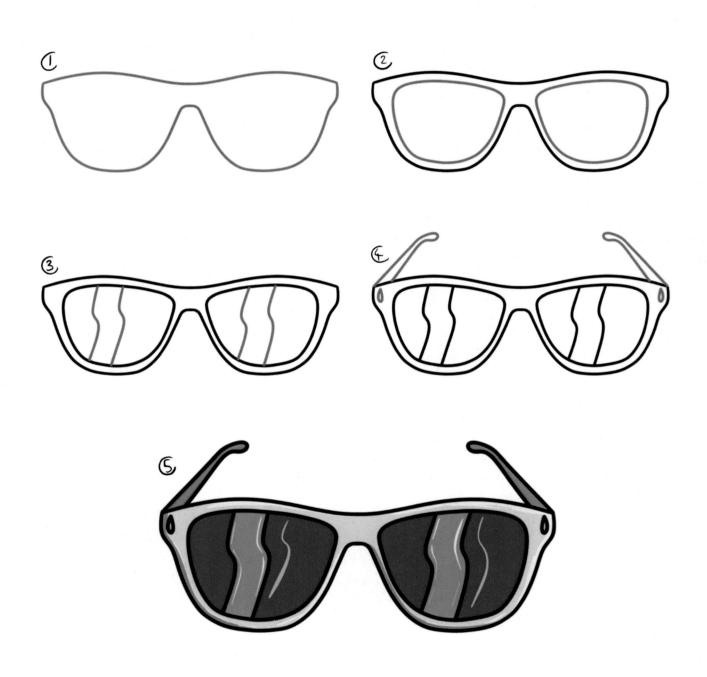

ROBOT

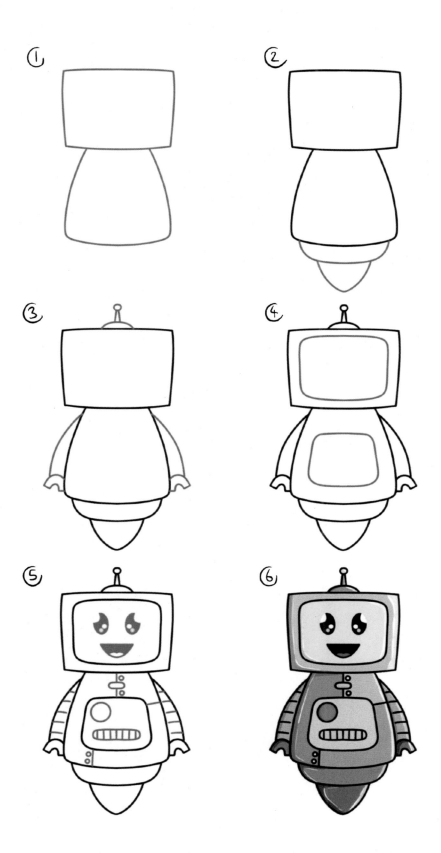

CACTUS

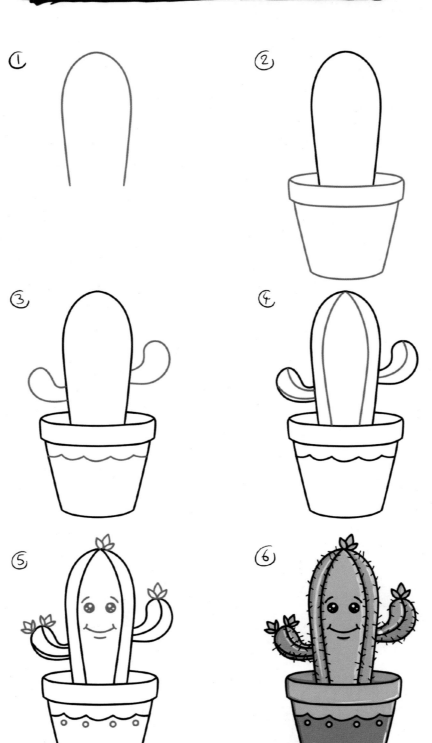

TREE

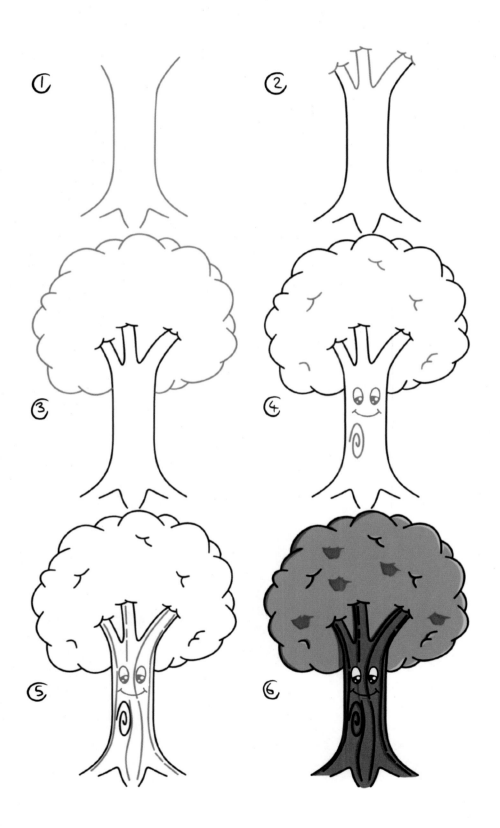

CAR

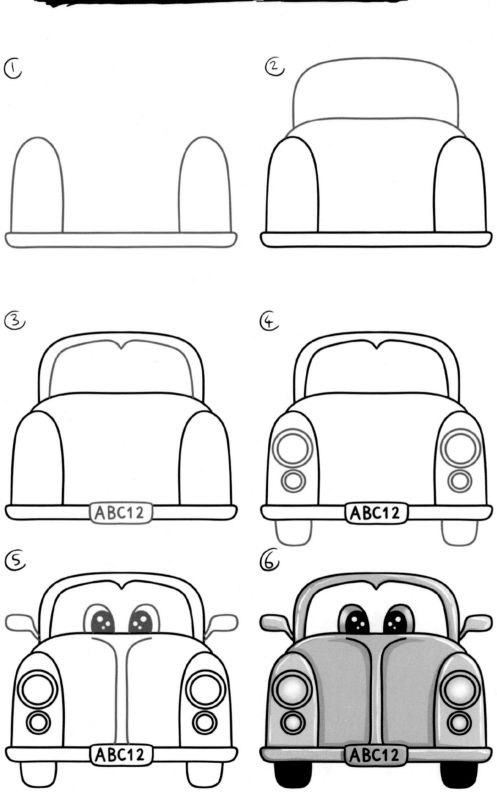

COTTON CANDY

LOLLIPOP

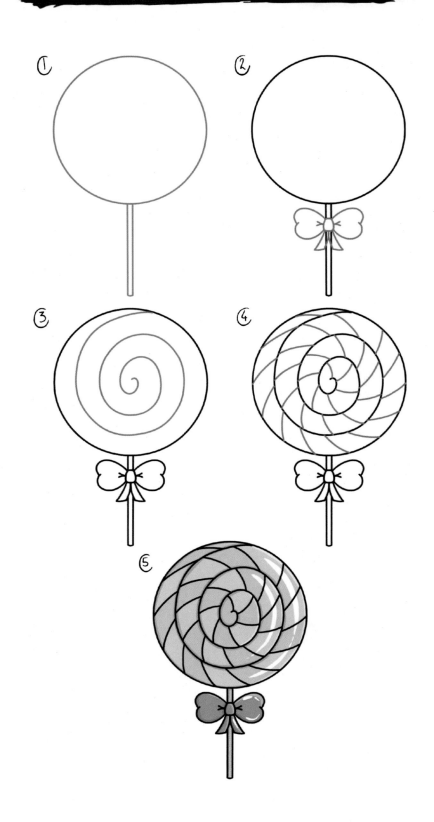

BLENDER

DONUT

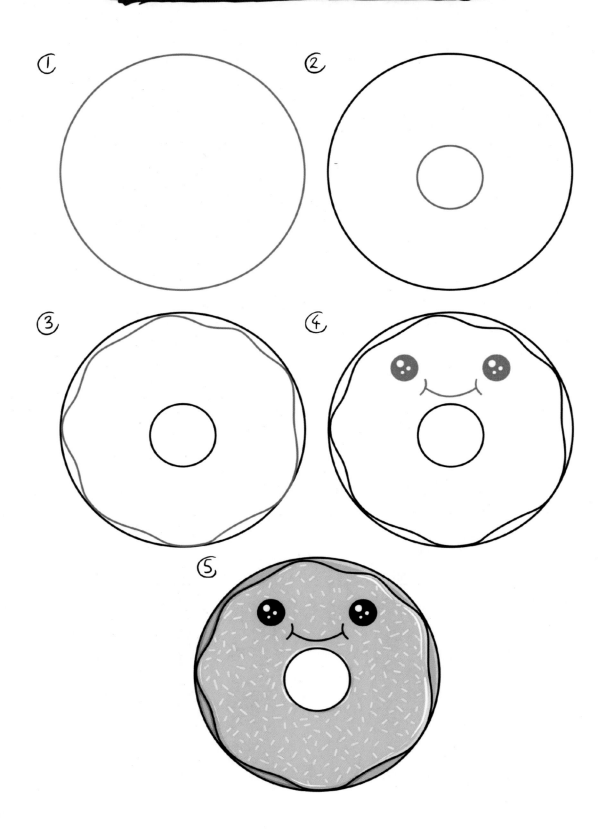

CHICK

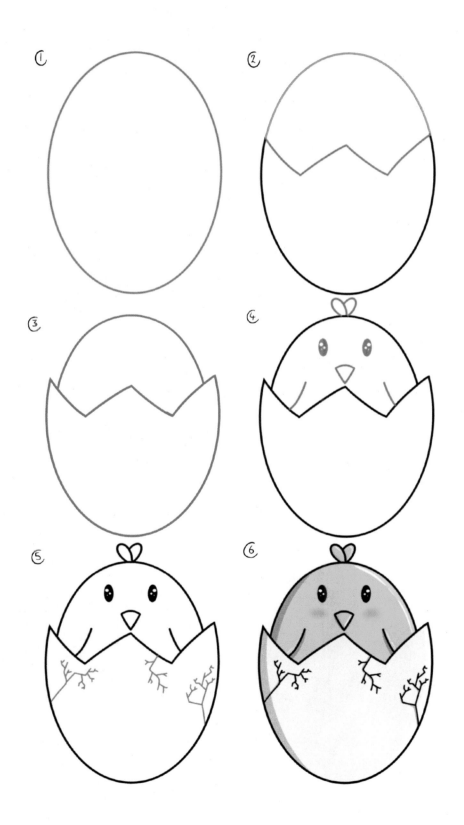

BEE

① ② ③ ④ ⑤ ⑥

MILK & COOKIES

PUPPY

CAMERA

①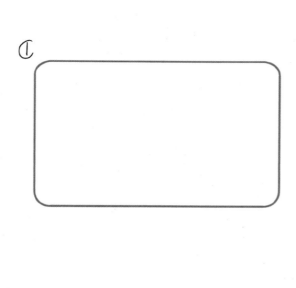

②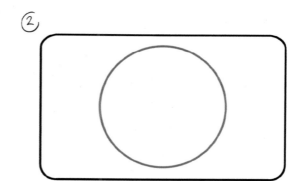

③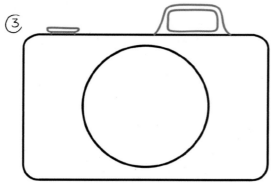

④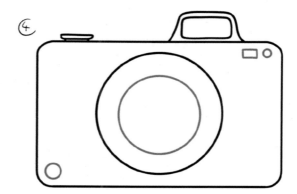

⑤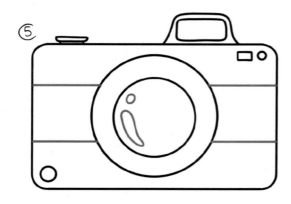

⑥

UNICORN

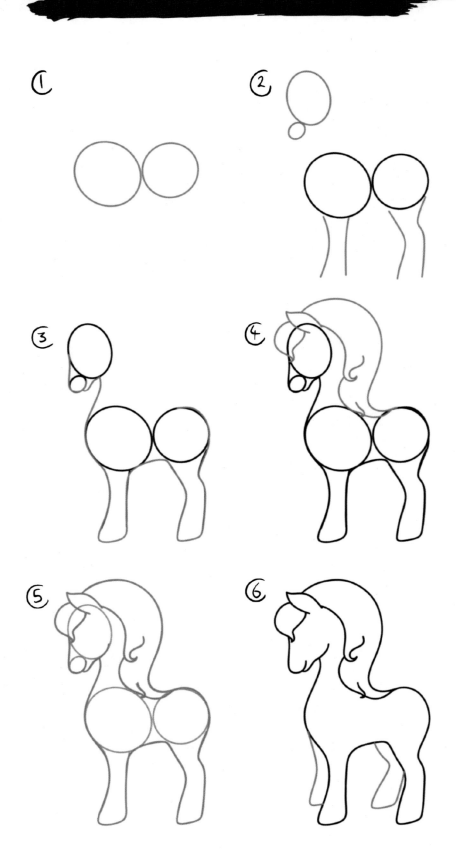

UNICORN

CAMP FIRE

PB&J

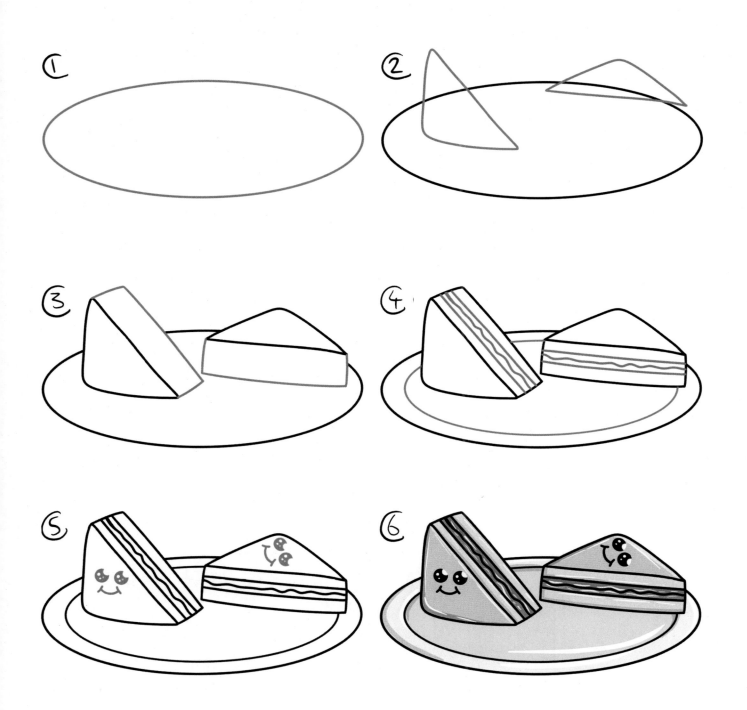

PHONE